THE WISDOM OF
Jesus

*Also edited by Owen Collins
and available from HarperCollins:*

The Definitive Bible Commentary

The Oral History of Christianity

Speeches that Changed the World

THE WISDOM OF Jesus

*Words of beauty
and truth for today*

edited by
OWEN COLLINS

Fount
An Imprint of HarperCollinsPublishers

Fount is an Imprint of
HarperCollins*Religious*
Part of HarperCollins*Publishers*
77–85 Fulham Palace Road, London w6 8jb

First published in Great Britain in 1999 by Fount

Compilation © 1999 Owen Collins

The Scripture quotations contained herein are from the New Revised Standard Version Bible, copyright © 1989, by the Division of Christian Education of the National Council of Churches of Christ in the U.S.A., and are used by permission. All rights reserved.

Scripture quotations marked 'KJV' are from the
King James (Authorized) Version.

Scripture quotations marked 'GNB' are from the Good News Bible published by the Bible Societies/HarperCollins*Publishers* Ltd,
© American Bible Society, 1966, 1971, 1976, 1992

1 3 5 7 9 10 8 6 4 2

Owen Collins asserts the moral right to be identified
as the editor of this work

A catalogue record for this book is available
from the British Library

ISBN 0 00 628131 1

Printed and bound in Great Britain by Woolnough Bookbinding Ltd,
Irthlingborough, Northamptonshire

CONDITIONS OF SALE

This book is sold subject to the condition that it shall not, by way of trade or otherwise, be lent, re-sold, hired out or otherwise circulated without the publisher's prior consent in any form of binding or cover other than that in which it is published and without a similar condition including this condition being imposed on the subsequent purchaser.

All rights reserved. No part of this publication may be reproduced, stored in a retrieval system, or transmitted, in any form or by any means, electronic, mechanical, photocopying, recording or otherwise, without the prior permission of the publishers.

Introduction

The wisdom of Jesus is timeless. His words have brought inspiration, hope and challenge to countless millions who have heard them over the past 2,000 years. Artists, writers, musicians, philosophers and scientists have drawn on the wisdom of Jesus. And ordinary people – from the poorest to the most privileged – have pondered on his words and found a startling new perspective on life.

The man who lived in an obscure corner of the Roman Empire has been more influential than any other individual in history. Even the calendar we use to measure time is fixed from his birth.

But who was he? He was not a military leader, held no political or religious office, wrote no books and never travelled far from his home. His words of wisdom were collected by his followers in the four accounts of his life known as the Gospels. Sometimes delightful, sometimes baffling, they are not easily dismissed by anyone who looks into the wisdom of Jesus.

Most of the sayings of Jesus quoted in this book are taken from the *New Revised Standard Version Bible* translation, but another version in everyday English – the *Good News Bible* (GNB) – is also used, as well as the much older, traditional *King James Version* (KJV).

Come unto me

Come unto me,
all ye that labour and
are heavy laden, and
I will give you rest.

MATTHEW 11:28 KJV

The Lord's Prayer

Our Father which art in heaven,
Hallowed be thy name.
Thy kingdom come.
Thy will be done in earth, as it is in heaven.
Give us this day our daily bread.
And forgive us our debts, as we forgive our
 debtors.
And lead us not into temptation,
but deliver us from evil.

MATTHEW 6:9–13 KJV

*B*elieving prayer

Whatever you
ask for in prayer
with faith, you
will receive.

MATTHEW 21:22

*A*sk, seek, knock

Ask, and it will be given to you;
search, and you will find;
knock, and the door will be opened for you.
For everyone who asks receives,
and everyone who searches finds,
and for everyone who knocks, the door will
be opened.

MATTHEW 7:7–8

Good gifts from heaven

Is there anyone among you who, if your child asks for bread, will give a stone? Or if the child asks for a fish, will give a snake? If you then, who are evil, know how to give good gifts to your children, how much more will your Father in heaven give good things to those who ask him!

MATTHEW 7:9–11

The golden rule

In everything do to others as you would have them do to you.

MATTHEW 7:12

Love your enemies

You have heard that it was said, 'You shall love your neighbour and hate your enemy.'

But I say to you, Love your enemies and pray for those who persecute you.

MATTHEW 5:43–5

A generous heart

Give, and it will be given to you ... for the measure you give will be the measure you get back.

Luke 6:38

Giving in secret

When you give
something to a
needy person,
do not make
a big show of it.

MATTHEW 6:2

Forgive

If you forgive others
the wrongs they have done
to you, your heavenly Father
will also forgive you.

MATTHEW 6:14–15 GNB

Forgiveness and love

The one to whom
little is forgiven,
loves little.

Luke 7:47

I am the truth

I am the way,
and the truth,
and the life.

JOHN 14:6

Truth and freedom

The truth will make you free.

JOHN 8:32

The bread of life

Whoever comes to me will never be hungry, and whoever believes in me will never be thirsty.

JOHN 6:35

*M*ore *to life than bread*

One does not
live by bread
alone.

MATTHEW 4:4

The light

I am the light
of the world.
Whoever follows me
will never walk in
darkness.

JOHN 8:12

I am the gate

I am the gate for the sheep ...
Whoever enters by me will
be saved, and will come in
and go out and find pasture.

JOHN 10:7,9

*A*bundant life

I came that
they may have life,
and have it
abundantly.

JOHN 10:10

The good shepherd

I am the good shepherd. The good shepherd lays down his life for the sheep ...

JOHN 10:11

Searching for one lost sheep

Which one of you, having a hundred sheep and losing one of them, does not leave the ninety-nine in the wilderness and go after the one that is lost until he finds it?

When he has found it, he lays it on his shoulders and rejoices. And when he comes home, he calls together his friends and neighbours, saying to them, 'Rejoice with me, for I have found my sheep that was lost.'

Just so, I tell you, there will be more joy in heaven over one sinner who repents than over ninety-nine righteous people who need no repentance.

LUKE 15:4–7

Life

I am the
resurrection
and the life.

JOHN 11:25

Life, *and not death*

Those who believe in me,
even though they die,
will live, and everyone
who lives and believes in
me will never die.

JOHN 11:26

The vine

A branch cannot bear fruit by itself; it can do so only if it remains in the vine. In the same way you cannot bear fruit unless you remain in me.

JOHN 15:4 GNB

*A*bide with me

If you abide in me, and
my words abide in you,
ask for whatever you wish,
and it will be done for you.

JOHN 15:7

No greater love

No one has greater
love than this,
to lay down one's life
for one's friends.

JOHN 15:13

*G*iving

It is
more blessed
to give
than to receive.

ACTS 20:35

An eye for an eye

You have heard that it was said, 'An eye for an eye and a tooth for a tooth.' But I say to you, Do not resist an evildoer. But if anyone strikes you on the right cheek, turn the other also.

MATTHEW 5:38–9

*T*he second mile

If anyone wants to sue you and take your coat, give your cloak as well; and if anyone forces you to go one mile, go also the second mile. Give to everyone who begs from you, and do not refuse anyone who wants to borrow from you.

MATTHEW 5:40–42

Treasures

Do not store up for yourselves treasures on earth, where moth and rust consume and where thieves break in and steal; but store up for yourselves treasures in heaven ... For where your treasure is, there your heart will be also.

MATTHEW 6:19–21

The choice: God or wealth?

No one can serve two masters; for a slave will either hate the one and love the other, or be devoted to the one and despise the other. You cannot serve God and wealth.

MATTHEW 6:24

*T*rusting God

All things
can be done
for the one
who believes.

MARK 9:23

Mustard seed faith

If you had faith the size of a mustard seed, you could say to this mulberry tree, 'Be uprooted and planted in the sea,' and it would obey you.

LUKE 17:6

*L*ook at the birds

Therefore I tell you, do not worry about your life, what you will eat or what you will drink, or about your body, what you will wear. Is not life more than food, and the body more than clothing? Look at the birds of the air; they neither sow nor reap nor gather into barns, and yet your heavenly Father feeds them. Are you not of more value than they?

MATTHEW 6:25–6

Wild flowers

Look how the wild flowers grow: they do not work or make clothes for themselves. But I tell you that not even King Solomon with all his wealth had clothes as beautiful as one of these flowers.

MATTHEW 6:28–9 GNB

Do not judge

Do not judge, so that you may not be judged. For with the judgement you make you will be judged, and the measure you give will be the measure you get.

MATTHEW 7:1–2

The speck and the log

Why do you see the speck in your neighbour's eye, but do not notice the log in your own eye? Or how can you say to your neighbour, 'Let me take the speck out of your eye,' while the log is in your own eye? You hypocrite, first take the log out of your own eye, and then you will see clearly to take the speck out of your neighbour's eye.

MATTHEW 7:3–5

A sword, not peace

Do not think that I have come to bring peace to the earth; I have not come to bring peace, but a sword.

Matthew 10:34

Deeds, not words

Not everyone who says to me, 'Lord, Lord,' will enter the kingdom of heaven, but only one who does the will of my Father in heaven.

MATTHEW 7:21

*S*alt

You are
like salt
for all
mankind.

MATTHEW 5:13 GNB

Light

You are
like light
for the whole
world.

Matthew 5:14 gnb

Let your light shine

Your light must shine before people,
so that they will see the good things you do
and praise your Father in heaven.

MATTHEW 5:16 GNB

The poor in spirit

Blessed are the
poor in spirit:
for theirs is the
kingdom of heaven.

MATTHEW 5:3 KJV

Mourning

Blessed are they
that mourn:
for they shall be
comforted.

MATTHEW 5:4 KJV

The meek

Blessed are the meek:
for they shall inherit
the earth.

MATTHEW 5:5 KJV

*H*ungry for God

Blessed are they
which do hunger and thirst
after righteousness:
for they shall be filled.

MATTHEW 5:6 KJV

The merciful

Blessed are the
merciful:
for they shall
obtain mercy.

MATTHEW 5:7 KJV

The pure in heart

Blessed are the
pure in heart:
for they shall
see God.

MATTHEW 5:8 KJV

The peacemakers

Blessed are the peacemakers:
for they shall be called
the children of God.

Matthew 5:9 kjv

Persecution

Blessed are they which are persecuted for righteousness' sake: for theirs is the kingdom of heaven.

    Blessed are ye, when men shall revile you, and persecute you, and shall say all manner of evil against you falsely, for my sake. Rejoice, and be exceeding glad: for great is your reward in heaven: for so persecuted they the prophets which were before you.

MATTHEW 5:10–12 KJV

*T*he kingdom of God

Let the little children come to me; do not stop them; for it is to such as these that the kingdom of God belongs. Truly I tell you, whoever does not receive the kingdom of God as a little child will never enter it.

MARK 10:14–15

Born again

No one can see the Kingdom of God unless he is born again.

JOHN 3:3 GNB

No resting place

Foxes have holes, and birds of the air have nests; but the Son of Man has nowhere to lay his head.

LUKE 9:58

Don't look back

No one who puts a hand
to the plough and
looks back is fit for
the kingdom of God.

LUKE 9:62

Death to life

Anyone who hears my word and believes him who sent me has eternal life, and does not come under judgement, but has passed from death to life.

JOHN 5:24

*L*ight has come

And this is the judgement, that the light has come into the world, and people loved darkness rather than light because their deeds were evil. For all who do evil hate the light and do not come to the light, so that their deeds may not be exposed. But those who do what is true come to the light, so that it may be clearly seen that their deeds have been done in God.

JOHN 3:19–21

Whom to fear

I tell you, my friends, do not fear those who kill the body, and after that can do nothing more. But I will warn you whom to fear: fear him who, after he has killed, has authority to cast into hell.

LUKE 12:4–5

*S*parrows

Are not five sparrows sold for two pennies? Yet not one of them is forgotten in God's sight. But even the hairs of your head are all counted. Do not be afraid; you are of more value than many sparrows.

Luke 12:6–7

A *stumbling-block*

If any of you put a stumbling-block before one of these little ones who believe in me, it would be better for you if a great millstone were fastened around your neck and you were drowned in the depth of the sea.

MATTHEW 18:6

Compassion

You can be sure that whoever gives even a drink of cold water to one of the least of these my followers because he is my follower, will certainly receive a reward.

MATTHEW 10:42 GNB

*S*erving one another

You call me Teacher and Lord – and you are right, for that is what I am. So if I, your Lord and Teacher, have washed your feet, you also ought to wash one another's feet. For I have set you an example, that you also should do as I have done to you.

JOHN 13:13–15

*H*umility

For everyone who makes himself great will be humbled, and everyone who humbles himself will be made great.

Luke 14:11

Love for the world

For God so loved the world that he gave his only Son, so that everyone who believes in him may not perish but may have eternal life.

JOHN 3:16

Belief in Jesus

This is the work of God, that you believe in him whom he has sent ...

This is indeed the will of my Father, that all who see the Son and believe in him may have eternal life; and I will raise them up on the last day.

JOHN 6:29,40

A challenging call

If any want to become my followers, let them deny themselves and take up their cross and follow me.

MARK 8:34

Gaining the whole world

For those who want to save their life will lose it, and those who lose their life for my sake, and for the sake of the gospel, will save it. For what will it profit them to gain the whole world and forfeit their life? Indeed, what can they give in return for their life?

MARK 8:35–7

Words without actions

Why do you call me, 'Lord, Lord,' and yet don't do what I tell you? Anyone who comes to me and listens to my words and obeys them – I will show you what he is like ...

LUKE 6:46–7 GNB

A house without foundations

... He is like a man who, in building his house, dug deep and laid the foundation on rock. The river overflowed and hit that house but could not shake it, because it was well built. But anyone who hears my words and does not obey them is like a man who built his house without laying a foundation; when the flood hit that house it fell at once – and what a terrible crash that was!

Luke 6:48–9 GNB

Godless teachers

Every plant that my heavenly Father has not planted will be uprooted ... They are blind guides of the blind. And if one blind person guides another, both will fall into a pit.

MATTHEW 15:13-14

*C*orruption

What comes out of the mouth proceeds from the heart, and this is what defiles. For out of the heart come evil intentions, murder, adultery, fornication, theft, false witness, slander. These are what defile a person.

MATTHEW 15:18–20

Not to be served but to serve

The Son of Man came not
to be served but to serve,
and to give his life
a ransom for many.

Matthew 20:28

Faithful service

Whoever serves me must follow me, and where I am, there will my servant be also. Whoever serves me, the Father will honour.

JOHN 12:26

The baggage of wealth

It is much harder for a rich person to enter the Kingdom of God than for a camel to go through the eye of a needle.

MATTHEW 19:24 GNB

No limits

For with God everything is possible.

MATTHEW 19:26

Jesus' family

Who are my mother and my brothers? And looking at those who sat around him, he said, Here are my mother and my brothers! Whoever does the will of God is my brother and sister and mother.

MARK 3:33–5

For or against?

Whoever is not
with me is against me,
and whoever does not
gather with me
scatters.

LUKE 11:23

*A*uthority

Render to Caesar the
things that are Caesar's,
and to God the
things that are God's.

MARK 12:17 GNB

The sabbath

The sabbath was made for humankind, and not humankind for the sabbath; so the Son of Man is lord even of the sabbath.

MARK 2:27–8

The first will be last

But many who are
first will be last,
and the
last will be first.

MATTHEW 19:30

Who needs a doctor?

Those who are well have no need of a physician, but those who are sick; I have come to call not the righteous but sinners to repentance.

LUKE 5:31–2

*D*on't be afraid

Do not be afraid,
little flock, for it is
your Father's good
pleasure to give you
the kingdom.

LUKE 12:32

*G*iving and saving

Sell all your belongings and give money to the poor. Provide for yourselves purses that don't wear out, and save your riches in heaven.

LUKE 12:33

*O*pen the door

Behold, I stand at the door, and knock: if any man hear my voice, and open the door, I will come in to him, and will sup with him, and he with me.

REVELATION 3:20 KJV

The narrow gate

Enter the narrow gate; for the gate is wide and the road is easy that leads to destruction, and there are many who take it. For the gate is narrow and the road is hard that leads to life, and there are few who find it.

MATTHEW 7:13–14

Troubled hearts

Do not let your
hearts be troubled.
Believe in God,
believe also in me.

JOHN 14:1

In my Father's house

In my Father's house there are many dwelling-places. If it were not so, would I have told you that I go to prepare a place for you? And if I go and prepare a place for you, I will come again and will take you to myself, so that where I am, there you may be also.

JOHN 14:2–3

*J*esus predicts his death

See, we are going up to Jerusalem, and the Son of Man will be handed over to the chief priests and scribes, and they will condemn him to death; then they will hand him over to the Gentiles to be mocked and flogged and crucified; and on the third day he will be raised.

MATTHEW 20:18–19

Jerusalem, Jerusalem!

Jerusalem, Jerusalem! You kill the prophets and stone the messengers God has sent you! How many times have I wanted to put my arms round all your people, just as a hen gathers her chicks under her wings, but you would not let me!

MATTHEW 23:37 GNB

Peace

I have said this to you, so that in me you may have peace. In the world you face persecution. But take courage; I have conquered the world!

JOHN 16:33

Peace I leave with you

Peace I leave with you; my peace I give to you. I do not give to you as the world gives. Do not let your hearts be troubled, and do not let them be afraid.

JOHN 14:27

Love God

The first [commandment] is, 'Hear, O Israel: the Lord our God, the Lord is one; you shall love the Lord your God with all your heart, and with all your soul, and with all your mind, and with all your strength.'

Mark 12:29–30

Love your neighbour

The second [commandment] is this, 'You shall love your neighbour as yourself.'

MARK 12:31

Loved by Jesus

As the Father
has loved me,
so have I loved you;
abide in my love.

JOHN 15:9

Love one another

This is my commandment, that you love one another, as I have loved you.

JOHN 15:12

For I was hungry ...

I was hungry and you gave me food, I was thirsty and you gave me something to drink, I was a stranger and you welcomed me, I was naked and you gave me clothing, I was sick and you took care of me, I was in prison and you visited me.

MATTHEW 25:35–6

The least of these

Truly I tell you, just as you did it to one of the least of these who are members of my family, you did it to me.

MATTHEW 25:40

Freedom

So if the Son
makes you free,
you will be free
indeed.

JOHN 8:36

The Spirit of the Lord is upon me

The Spirit of the Lord is upon me,
   because he has anointed me
      to bring good news to the poor.
He has sent me to proclaim release to the captives
and recovery of sight to the blind,
      to let the oppressed go free,
to proclaim the year of the Lord's favour.

LUKE 4:18–19

*G*lobal salvation

Indeed, God did not send the Son into the world to condemn the world, but in order that the world might be saved through him.

JOHN 3:17

This is eternal life

And this is eternal life,
that they may know you,
the only true God, and
Jesus Christ whom you
have sent.

JOHN 17:3

*N*ot alone

For where two
or three are gathered
in my name, I am there
among them.

MATTHEW 18:20

The harvest

The harvest is plentiful,
but the labourers are few;
therefore ask the Lord of the
harvest to send out labourers
into his harvest.

LUKE 10:2

*Y*our heavenly Father knows

So do not start worrying: 'Where will my food come from? or my drink? or my clothes?' (These are the things the pagans are always concerned about.) Your Father in heaven knows that you need all these things.

MATTHEW 6:31–2 GNB

Do not worry about tomorrow

Instead, be concerned above everything else with the Kingdom of God and with what he requires of you, and he will provide you with all these other things. So do not worry about tomorrow; it will have enough worries of its own. There is no need to add to the troubles each day brings.

MATTHEW 6:33–4 GNB

Like sheep among wolves

See, I am sending you out like sheep into the midst of wolves; so be wise as serpents and innocent as doves.

MATTHEW 10:16

A *public believer*

If anyone declares publicly that he belongs to me, I will do the same for him before my Father in heaven.

Matthew 10:32

*T*houghts

You have heard that it was said, 'You shall not commit adultery.' But I say to you that everyone who looks at a woman with lust has already committed adultery with her in his heart.

Matthew 5:27–8

A radical prescription

If your right eye causes you to sin, tear it out and throw it away; it is better for you to lose one of your members than for your whole body to be thrown into hell.

MATTHEW 5:29

Streams of water

Whoever is thirsty should come to me and drink. As the scripture says, 'Whoever believes in me, streams of life-giving water will pour out from his heart.'

JOHN 7:37–8 GNB

Thirst quenched

Whoever drinks this water will be thirsty again, but whoever drinks the water that I will give him will never be thirsty again. The water that I will give him will become in him a spring which will provide him with life-giving water and give him eternal life.

JOHN 4:13–14 GNB

How not to pray

When you pray, do not be like the hypocrites! They love to stand up and pray in the houses of worship and on the street corners, so that everyone will see them. I assure you, they have already been paid in full.

MATTHEW 6:5 GNB

How to pray

But when you pray, go to your room, close the door, and pray to your Father, who is unseen. And your Father, who sees what you do in private, will reward you.

When you pray, do not use a lot a meaningless words, as the pagans do, who think that their gods will hear them because their prayers are long. Do not be like them. Your Father already knows what you need before you ask him.

MATTHEW 6:6–8 GNB

From the cross

Forgive them, Father!
They don't know
what they are doing.

LUKE 23:34 GNB

To a dying thief

I promise you that today
you will be in Paradise
with me.

LUKE 23:43 GNB

A word for Mary and John

Jesus saw his mother and the disciple he loved standing there [at the foot of the cross]; so he said to his mother, 'He is your son.'

Then he said to the disciple, 'She is your mother.' From that time the disciple took her to live in his home.

JOHN 19:26–7 GNB

Jesus' last words

At about three o'clock Jesus cried out with a loud shout, '*Eli, Eli, lema sabachthani?*' which means, 'My God, my God, why did you abandon me?' MATTHEW 27:46 GNB

I am thirsty. JOHN 19:28 GNB

Father! In your hands I place my spirit! LUKE 23:46 GNB

It is finished! JOHN 19:30 GNB

Fishers of men

Follow me, and
I will make you
fish for people.

Matthew 4:19

Go ... and make disciples

All authority in heaven and on earth has been given to me. Go therefore and make disciples of all nations, baptizing them in the name of the Father and of the Son and of the Holy Spirit, and teaching them to obey everything that I have commanded you.

MATTHEW 28:18–20a

Jesus' presence

And remember,
I am with you always,
to the end of the age.

MATTHEW 28:20b